Motorhome Marilyn

Ben Weatherill

methuen | drama

LONDON · NEW YORK · OXFORD · NEW DELHI · SYDNEY

METHUEN DRAMA

Bloomsbury Publishing Plc, 50 Bedford Square, London, WC1B 3DP, UK
Bloomsbury Publishing Inc, 1359 Broadway, New York, NY 10018, USA
Bloomsbury Publishing Ireland, 29 Earlsfort Terrace, Dublin 2,
D02 AY28, Ireland

BLOOMSBURY, METHUEN DRAMA and the Methuen
Drama logo are trademarks of Bloomsbury Publishing Plc.

First published in Great Britain 2025

A catalogue record for this book is available from the British Library.

A catalog record for this book is available from the Library of Congress.

ISBN: PB: 978-1-3505-9991-8
ePDF: 978-1-3505-9992-5
eBook: 978-1-3505-9993-2

Series: Modern Plays

Typeset by Mark Heslington Ltd, Scarborough, North Yorkshire
Printed and bound in Great Britain

For product safety related questions contact
productsafety@bloomsbury.com.

To find out more about our authors and books visit
www.bloomsbury.com and sign up for our newsletters.

Acknowledgments

Firstly, thank you to Joshua Beaumont, Matthew Emeny and The Production Garden for keeping the wheels of the motorhome turning and the headlights on. Big love to ASJ, whose direction steers us through sequins, sorrow and snakes with extraordinary care. And to Michelle Collins – for trusting me with this twisted, tragicomic tale and for breathing such unforgettable life into Denise.

Cheers to Sam Baxter, whose sound design made the desert sing (and slither); to Joe Taylor for costume design; and to Twinkle, especially for hunting down so many fantastic props.

This beautiful playtext is down to the hard work of Dom O'Hanlon, Sophie Campbell and the extraordinary team at Methuen Drama. And to everyone at the Gilded Balloon – thank you for giving the show such a warm and fabulous home.

I'm deeply grateful to Giles Smart and Lee Byrne at United Agents for their tireless support, and to the late Stewart Permutt, whose original spark helped shape this journey.

And lastly, thank you, Marilyn Monroe. For the grit, the heartbreak, and the stardust.

The production of this play is dedicated to Stewart Permutt who we sadly lost in 2023. Stewart was a great friend and writer whose legacy we hope we have honoured with this show.

Cast and Creative Team

Denise/Original Idea – Michelle Collins

Writer – Ben Weatherill

Director – Alexandra Spencer-Jones

Design – The Production Garden

Costume Design – Joe Taylor

Sound Designer – Sam Baxter

Company Manager – Anna-Lisa Marie

Press – Alison Duguid

Producer – Joshua Beaumont

Producer – Matthew Emeny

Production Co-ordinator – Mirella Lloussi

Executive Producer – Huw Allen

Thanks

Andrew Lancel, Harriet Thorpe, Mike Davison, Katie Finch, Tilley Sheridan, Karen and Katy Koren and all at Gilded Balloon, Rebecca Pitt, Michael Wharley and the Marilyn Monroe fans who have gifted us such incredible items of Marilyn memorabilia.

Content warning: this play includes strong language and swearing.

Cast

Denise – Michelle Collins

Michelle started out her career in youth theatre and at the age of 18 was turned down by every single drama school, never one to take no for an answer she pursued her dream.

She is an accomplished actress in TV, Stage and film also a writer and a producer.

She has appeared in *Eastenders* and *Coronation Street* two of Britain's best loved soaps but is also a very versatile performer appearing in *Dr Who, Miss Marple, Real Women, Sunburn, 2000 Acres of Skye, Perfect, Ella and The Mothers, Can't Buy Me Love, Death in Paradise, The Last Detective, The Family Man, Queens of Mystery, The Dumping Ground*, the acclaimed *Illustrated Mum* which won 2 BAFTAs and an international Emmy.

Musicals such as: *Chitty Chitty Bang Bang, Daddy Cool, Thoroughly Modern Millie, Never Forget.*

Theatre includes: *Rattle Of A Simple Man, Calendar Girls, My Dads Gap Year, A Dark Night in Dalston, The Glass Supper, How Love is Spelt, Romeo and Juliet* and *Cluedo* and many more.

Films include: *Personal Services, Black Road, My House, Stephen, soon to be self-storage.*

This play is very close to Michelle's heart and she dedicates it to her dear friend Stewart Permutt.

Michelle is also a co producer on *Motorhome Marilyn* alongside Joshua Beaumont and Matthew Emeny for The Production Garden.

Michelle is London born and bred, born in Hackney and brought up in Islington and very proud of it.

She is a campaigner for women rights, ambassador for Barnardos, Chicken Shed Theatre, North London Hospice and supports the @lgbtq+ community.

She has her own production company called it Worx.

This is her first Edinburgh show.

Creative Team

Writer – Ben Weatherill

Ben Weatherill is a playwright from the East Midlands. His plays include *Chicken Dust* (Finborough Theatre/Curve), *Jellyfish* (Bush Theatre/National Theatre), *Frank and Percy* (Theatre Royal Windsor/Bath/The Other Palace), and *Motorhome Marilyn*. He is currently developing a slate of original television projects and writes on *Death in Paradise* (BBC). He is passionate about nurturing new voices, big characters, and creating work that connects across communities.

Director – Alexandra Spencer-Jones

ASJ is the Artistic Director of international touring ensemble Action To The Word for whom she created the award-winning all-male adaptation of *A Clockwork Orange* (Soho Theatre, The Park Theatre, New World Stages Broadway), *Dracula* (Arts Theatre), *Macbeth, Romeo & Juliet, A Midsummer Night's Dream* (NT Riverside), *The Lost Boy* (Pleasance), *Chopped Logic* (Shakespeare North) and her award-winning musical *Constance & Sinestra* and *The Cabinet of Screams* (New Wimbledon). Other Directing: *Gobsmacked!* (Southbank Centre, International Tour), *A Generous Lover* (International Tour), *Legally Blonde* (Assembly), *Women Beware Women* (CPT), *Godspell* (Assembly), *Rent* (Birmingham Hippodrome). For Greenwich Theatre: *The Grinning Man, Return To The Forbidden Planet, All Day Permanent Red* (Royal Court), *Pains of Youth* (Master Shipbuilder's Theatre), *City of Angels* (Stratford), *Spring Awakening* (Stratford Circus). For RCS: *Bat Boy!, Street Scene, Sweeney Todd, Legally Blonde* and *Sweet Charity* (RCS). She is currently directing *Carousel* for NYMT.

As Associate Director: *Bend it Like Beckham* (West End), *Stepping Out* (UK Tour). For Grange Opera: *Peter Grimes* and *Oliver!, Hope* (Royal Court) and *La Perichole* (Garsington

Opera). As Assistant Director: *The Wizard of Oz* (London Palladium). She is currently Associate Director of Six Worldwide. She is represented by Simon Blakey of The Agency.

Costume Designer – Joe Taylor

Joe Taylor is a costume and fashion designer from East Sussex. Studying fashion at the University of Brighton, his graduate menswear collection was shortlisted for innovation award.

Costume design work includes: *EastEnders* (BBC Studios), *Red White & Royal Blue* (Crowd costume – History Huh) and *Motorhome Marilyn*

Productions includes: *Beyond Paradise* (Red Planet Pictures), *Heartstopper* (See Saw Films), *Cruella* (Badduns Productions for Disney), *Cuffs* (Tiger Aspect), *Poluito* (Glyndebourne Opera House)

Fashion houses include: *McQ* (Alexander McQueen)

He is passionate about sustainability in design and the use of repurposing materials to offer a new lease of life to unwanted materials, regularly the foundation of all his recent creative work.

Sound Designer – Sam Baxter

Sam is a sound designer and performer from Leeds.

Sound design includes: *A Shoddy Detective & The Art of Deception* (Mercury Colchester, UK Tour & Ed Fringe); *Parody of the Rings* (Ed Fringe); *Why I Stuck a Flare Up My A**e For England* (Southwark Playhouse, UK Tour, Edinburgh & Adelaide Fringe); *You Are Going to Die* (Southwark Playhouse); *A Manchester Anthem* (Ed Fringe & Riverside Studios); *Putrid Beauty* (Actors East); *The Cosmonauts Last Message...* (Oxford School of Drama).

Company Stage Manager – Anna-Lisa Marie aka 'Twinkle'

Since gaining a degree in Stage Management from RWCMD and a Post Graduate Diploma in Acting from ALRA , Anna-Lisa has enjoyed a wide and varied career as an all-round 'theatre fairy' working both nationally and internationally. She has held a number of job titles from Company Stage Manager to Head of Wardrobe as well as Producer, Director and Writer on her own shows, Anna-Lisa's also an accomplished costume character artiste who would like to dedicate her involvement with *Motorhome Marilyn* to her beautiful friends, Kris Andersson and Dixie Longate who she first met at the Edinburgh Fringe back in 2022.

Press – Alison Duguid

Originally from Scotland, Alison Duguid brings over 25 years of experience in arts and not-for-profit communications to her role as a Press and PR Consultant. Following her degree in English and Drama from Queen Mary and Westfield College, University of London, and the Central School of Speech and Drama, Alison worked as a musician before kicking off her theatre career at Regent's Park Open Air Theatre. She has since worked in press, website and publications management for a diverse range of organisations with highlights including managing press for the Society of London Theatre, leading PR campaigns for major West End and touring productions and working in family, regional and Fringe theatre, including in-house venue roles. Beyond the arts, Alison has held senior communications roles within the charity and public sectors, including at The Prince's Charities at the Royal Household, and the Millennium Commission. She currently serves as a Trustee of the Charlie Kristensen Foundation promoting anti-bulling, acceptance and access to the arts for young people.

The Production Garden – Producer and General Manager

Joshua Beaumont – Producer

Matthew Emeny – Producer

Mirella Lloussi – Production Co-ordinator

Huw Allen – Executive Producer

The Production Garden is an Award-Winning Theatre and Event Production company co-founded by Joshua Beaumont and Matthew Emeny.

TPG Productions include: Tony and Olivier Award winning *ART* by Yasmina Reza starring Seann Walsh (UK Tour), *Pride and Prejudice* (*Sort Of)* by Isobel McArthur (CAA, Toronto – North American Premiere), *Awake My Soul: The Mumford and Sons Story* (UK Tour), *Why I Stuck A Flare Up My Arse For England* (2025 Offie Award Winner, Adelaide Fringe Award Winner, Holden Street Theatre Award Winner, Southwark Playhouse, UK Tour, Australia), Sebastian Faulks *Birdsong* (UK Tour and Alexandra Palace), *A Shoddy Detective and the Art of Deception* (UK Tour), *A Shoddy Christmas Carol* (Lichfield Garrick Theatre and UK Tour), *Jenny Ryan: Out Of The Box* (UK Tour), Co-Producer on *The Croft* by Ali Miles (UK Tour) and *Murder at Midnight* by Torben Betts (UK Tour).

Forthcoming Productions include: *Parody of The Rings* (Edinburgh Fringe Festival), Michael Morpurgo's *Private Peaceful* adapted and directed by Simon Reade (UK Tour), Seann Walsh in *Chaplin* by James Kettle (Edinburgh) and *Disenchanted The Musical* (London and UK Tour).

The Production Garden also creates theatrical events including The Garden Theatre Festival; Bath's only outdoor theatre event, presenting a repertory theatre company bringing classic plays to a bespoke 400 seat theatre every summer to the gardens of the Holburne Museum and Father Christmas' Grotto at Milsom Place, Bath.

Motorhome Marilyn

Characters

Denise, *a sixty-year-old Marilyn Monroe impersonator, living and working around the Vegas Strip. She's originally from South End, and the American twang has never rubbed off on her.*

Setting

Denise's *motorhome. The Las Vegas strip. Present day.*

Marilyn Monroe memorabilia everywhere. In every nook and cranny.

Hoarder is the understatement of the century.

The trailer is packed to the rafters with Monroe memorabilia. The place isn't filthy or anything; she's houseproud. It's just that she can't throw anything away and has let her obsession get out of hand. It's now a museum, or a shrine, on wheels.

Two doors – one to the outside world and one to the tiny bathroom.

In the corner, there is a large vivarium containing **Bobby**, **Denise**'s *reticulated python, whom she talks to throughout.*

Scene One – *"Patsy, Trisha and Misty"*

Lights up on **Denise***'s motorhome. Night.*

Denise *enters, dressed in a coat and sunglasses. She takes off the coat – underneath, she's dressed as Marilyn Monroe in the classic white halter neck.*

Relieved to be home, she plonks herself down, takes the sunglasses off and puts them somewhere safe. She kicks her heels off. The soles of her feet are filthy. She rubs her tired soles.

Denise I was spat at by Captain America today. I know, not very gentlemanly, is it, Bobby? I've never, in my entire life, spat at another human being.

Captain America comes out of nowhere. To tell you the truth Bobby, anyone dressing up as a superhero in real life? Immediate dickhead. I know that's a bit rich coming from me. People have to earn a living pretending to be all kinds of people. I once met an Ellen DeGeneres impersonator – that must've been a tough gig.

Denise *pulls out a battered fan with Marilyn's face on it and begins wafting herself.*

Heat's disgusting tonight. Vegas makes me so uneasy when it's hot. Sequins scratch your skin, and the liquor's warm. Feels like predators can smell your sweat. The stench of your mistakes.

She puts the fan down.

Denise Should've paid to have that electric fan fixed. But I needed fabric. And don't you agree, the dress looks glorious?

She does a twirl in her outfit, but she notices a dark, red smudge on the dress. She spits on her finger, dabs at it.

She opens the window to the trailer.

I hope they're right and this breaks by Saturday. I always sleep like crap in a heatwave. But you shouldn't pray for a storm, should you, Bobby?

She rummages around and finds a pill container.

These new sleeping pills Vince got me.

She reads the back of the packet.

Lunesta. Terrible. S'posed to be able to knock out a horse. All they did was make me see one standing in the corner of the room! Had a lovely singing voice, though.

She pours a small handful, dry swallows them. She sits.

I just wanna close my eyes without feeling something there in the dark. Bet you wouldn't know anything about that, would you? Must be nice. Top of the food chain. Captain Dickhead wouldn't dare spit in your face.

To be fair, I've never understood the superhero thing. Terribly common. There's artistry to what I do. I'm real. Half-heartedly pouring yourself into a costume any pleb could buy on Amazon? It's vulgar.

That's why I sew all my own looks. Course it was Gran who taught me on her machine. It had dents in it from all the times she threw it at Grandad when the bobbin jammed. Think she gave me lessons to keep me quiet, but I was hooked. Marilyn stitched too, you know. Between takes. I read that.

But it's not just about *looking* like her. Plenty of people can do that. No, I've *'studied her voice'*. The mannerisms. It's all in the little glances – a pout, tilt of the head. It's a privilege to shed me, slip her skin on. When I'm Marilyn, I have the whole world at my fingertips . . . but she's also taught me you can't be fooled. You might hold it all in your hands, but it's still made of glass.

Beat.

Anyway, Captain Dickhead storms over, face like I'd pissed in his Cheerios. I've been working this corner all week cos there's a decent air vent, and it's good for business. Suddenly, he's saying I'm encroaching on his turf. I dunno, maybe I am. I've not done the tourist thing in a while. But you know how slow it's been. All the corporate stuff goes to lookalikes with TikTok followings now.

So, there I was. Dress billowing in a warm draft, worrying I was giving myself a yeast infection, but at least I'd been cleaning up. A hundred and sixty bucks in two hours, and it's not like Captain Dickhead owns the south end of the Strip, is it? I tell him I'm not moving.

That's when he starts yelling. And you haven't been sworn at 'til you've been cursed out by an entitled Yank. Aggressive. Territorial. Americans don't want anything taken away from them unless it's women's rights.

He gives me three seconds to move. Who does he think he is? I tell him, *'Over my dead body.'* Which I admit, is a stupid thing to say in Vegas. People get wiped out every day. My friend Mario? Shot in a Wendy's toilet. Totally embarrassing. It wasn't even a Shake Shack.

That's when I feel it hit the side of my face. Right here. Phlegm. Disgusting! Just misses my eye, thank God. I let out the biggest scream. And did anyone stop to help me? See if I the lady who'd just got gobbed on in the street was alright? Please. Those days are gone.

She chuckles to herself.

I contemplated gouging his eyes out. You can take the girl outta South End . . .

But I've just had a manicure, so, I think no – I'll find something you care about and kill that instead. Which brings me to your dinner, Bobby.

She gets a carrier bag out of her large (fake) Dior handbag. There's something dead, red and bloody sloshing around inside.

But she hears something outside. Her eyes flick toward the window.

Did you hear that?

She puts the bag down. She moves to the window. Waits. She closes it.

(*Turning back to* **Bobby**.) Probably nothing. Now, are you ready for tonight's special? It's justice, served cold.

After ten minutes pacing the pavement, trying to remember why I ever gave up smoking, I opt for the next best thing: coffee. I have a loyalty card at this cute little independent place – Starbucks.

I sit upstairs; it's quieter. Not only am I a woman in public, but I'm also dressed as Marilyn Monroe, so you can imagine the kind of shit men think's okay to say to me.

– Where's the bullet hole, baby?

– *Hey Cutie, can I show you my Oval Office?*

– Fuck me, all the drugs really did take their toll, didn't they?

You get tired, Bobby.

She gets up and walks over to the tank. She peers in through the glass.

I'm sorry, you've been alone for hours. And on your birthday, too. Thirteen. Such a big boy.

So, I'm upstairs at the Starbucks, and he comes in to use the bathroom. And sometimes you've gotta take the stage direction from the Universe.

He doesn't notice me tailing him to the bus stop. People must think I'm mad, wearing a coat and headscarf in this heat, but. I watch him through my sunglasses as he picks his nose and wipes it on the back of an old woman's seat.

He gets off near Spring Valley. I have to take my heels off as he walks fast and I don't wanna lose him. But I keep enough distance. The house is big. Must be his parents' place – he could never afford it.

A nice garden. Pool. Chickens in a coop. Clucking away – gorgeous feathers, all these different colours. I wait until it goes dark, and around nine o'clock, he comes out to feed the hens. I crouch in the bushes and watch as he coos to them. Penny. Trisha. Misty. They have names. It's very sweet, to be fair.

Beat.

I wait until he goes inside. Then I kill them all. Slit their throats. I do it cleanly; try not to spook them. I know those poor chickens weren't responsible for his actions, but it feels like justice. Somehow, to me.

I write 'COCK-A-DOODLE-DICKHEAD' on the wall in blood. I pick the fattest one, I think that's Trisha, and I drive off. Perhaps they'll think a particularly literate bobcat has had its way with them.

She picks up the chicken from the bag with a pair of tongs.

Open wide. Here comes the airplane.

She dangles Trisha into the tank.

That's it. Who's a good boy?

*She feeds **Bobby** as she sings to him.*

Denise   *Happy birthday to you. Happy birthday to you. Happy birthday, my dear serpent. Happy birthday to you.*

*She watches **Bobby** eat. She should look satisfied. But she doesn't.*

Scene Two – *"Legends Reborn"*

Denise *bursts in, in a great mood but a little flustered.*

Denise   Bobby, code red! Visitor alert. You know I often talk to Vince – well, he's just caught me, musta seen me practically walking on air . . .

But what's he gonna think of the place? Eh? I s'pose he owns the site, but doesn't mean he gets to see inside, does it? Innocent enough maybe, suggesting we could meet here, but I don't think that's wise. He knows about the collection, but he's never actually *seen* it. Can't imagine he'd be thrilled about having sex in a Marilyn Monroe shrine on wheels. Not that anything intimate's definitely on the cards. But.

She grabs a bottle of Chanel No. 5, sprays it over herself like a fire extinguisher.

Although, what if Marilyn's the allure? Course he doesn't want *Denise* – he only ever sees the wig and warpaint, slinking in and out after dark. He probably wouldn't recognise me in the light, without all this. Who would? No. He can't come here.

She sits. Immediately up again, pacing.

Can he? It was his idea to celebrate. A few drinks, attack the dancefloor. Imagine that. I used to love the Red Barn when I first rolled into Vegas. It was this gay club on Tropicana, run by Loretta. A lesbian with hair so big it could house San Francisco. Every month, she'd host rodeos, these charity hayrides for folks living with AIDS. Everyone would show up bombed out of their brains and try to stay on the bucking bronco. The bottoms were unsurprisingly expert at riding that thing.

What I'd give to go back in time. Those boys used to eat me up.

She's suddenly sad. She picks up her mobile, starts typing a message.

I'll text Vince. Tell him it's a bad idea. Out on the strip? Please.

She hits send.

It was a nice thought. Healthy to live in a fantasy every now and then. Vince has been good to me the past few months. Never asked questions. But this? It's too close. You and me can celebrate on our own. Had plenty of practice.

Let's not dwell. Today's been a good day. An excellent day. And how many truly excellent days do you get in life? Six, seven? Less than ten, I reckon. And today was one of them.

I finally tracked down Joanie Fontaine. And yes, *that* Joanie Fontaine. Say her name and half of Vegas checks their lipstick. She started out at the Sahara, but turned a G-string and a smile into an empire.

And all the rumours are true! Joanie's putting her life's savings into a new revue at the Decadence. Not like the old tribute shows, this is gonna be classy. Live orchestra, velvet booths, and no lip-syncing. Each act's gonna have their own chapter – ten, fifteen minutes – a love letter to the golden era. With all the greats. Sinatra, Garland, Presley.

She's hit by a memory for a second. Pushes it aside quickly – moves on.

And I knew it. Told you, didn't I? Joanie's looking for a Marilyn.

She lets her imagination run away with her for a moment.

I could finally stop serenading sales reps. Begging for tips from bachelorette parties who think I'm Anna Nicole Smith. A real show, Bobby! A chance for my costumes to feel stage lights on their skin again.

I rang the casting director, but he just laughed. Said he'd seen my headshot and I was *'ageing like milk'*. I'm not a moron, I know they could go younger, but I've been Marilyn longer than most of these other girls have been alive. And that's a gift. I knew if I could just get to Joanie, she might see that.

'Course I've never forgotten when Marilyn found out John Huston was casting *The Asphalt Jungle*, she showed up, demanding he screen tested her. Turns out, Joanie gets oxygen facials at some bougie spa off Flamingo. I booked in for a clay wrap, the cheapest treatment I could find. Smelled like wet dog.

I think Joanie was quite surprised to find me in the changing rooms, half covered in mud. Took me too long to realise in life – it's never the best who get picked. Just the ones who march in like they belong.

I launched straight into a scene from *Bus Stop*. Marilyn plays a lounge singer, desperate to escape her dead-end existence. Bit on the nose, maybe. But sometimes you've gotta lean in, Bobby.

Denise *launches into a few iconic lines from the movie, where Cherie talks about feeling like she's spent her whole life running.*

She waited for me to finish, took a sip of her green juice and said: *'Fine. You can have an audition. I don't care if you're sixty or six hundred – make me believe.'*

And I will.

Scene Three – *"Matzo Balls and Matches"*

Morning. **Denise** *enters.*

Denise   Morning. I ended up butt naked on top of the sheets again.

It's quieter here, don't you think? Much better than that last dump we were at. Here, the sky's so clear you can see the stars. I thought about letting you out of your viv, so we could watch the universe spin. But maybe it's best you don't realise what you're missing out on. Wouldn't want you slithering off now, would I?

You ever think about how you'd survive in the wild, Bobby? I mean, you were never supposed to be trapped in here. You must crave fresh air. Dirt. The thrill of crushing something to death.

Beat.

There's a place in the San Gabriel Mountains. That's the best spot for stargazing. But we can never go back there.

A sudden bang on the motorhome door. **Denise***'s blood runs cold.*

Vince's Voice (*off*)   *Mail!*

Denise (*calling out*)   Oh! Thanks, Vince!

She wraps a dressing gown around her. She opens the motorhome door and picks up the mail. She squeals, excited.

Bobby! Look, I think it's here! Finally arrived. Where are the scissors?

She searches, locates them in her fruit bowl. Begins unwrapping it with great anticipation.

If this turns out to be your shedding supplements, I'm gonna be very upset.

She's got it open! Thrilled, she holds up the contents.

It's a vintage-style matchbook – red, slightly worn, with the Formosa Café logo stamped across the front in gold. She holds it up, reverent.

It's a matchbook from the Formosa Café. Isn't it beautiful? Look – still got a little scorch mark from where she struck one. It was the night she ordered the matzo balls just to tick Arthur Miller off.

His mother, Isadore, used to make matzo balls from scratch. She served them so often that one night, Marilyn asked, *'Isn't there any other part of the matzo you can eat?'* One joke about Arthur's mother doomed the marriage. Well, that and Arthur's raging alcoholism. That man was a drinker with a writing problem.

Once she finished the matzo balls, Marilyn struck a match from this very book, lit her cigarette, and declared the meal much tastier than his mother's. Arthur flipped the table as Marilyn ordered another Dom Perignon.

Denise *smiles proudly.*

I don't care if it's real. Now, where's the perfect spot?

She scans the motorhome.

You have to be careful with treasures, Bobby. Take care of them. There's too much light near the Moon of Baroda replica diamond. And beside the JFK action figure's no good. God, you need so much shelf space for history.

She makes room in a crowded area.

(*Scanning.*) Oh yes. Perfect. Next to the thing that started it all.

She places the matchbook down, picks up a cinema ticket.

Southend Odeon. Red velvet seats, Gran's smuggled mint imperials. I've told you before but you really woulda loved Gran. Always six steps ahead. Right about everything. Knew

Cody was trouble from the get-go. She always told me: *'The more I learn about men, the more I admire dogs.'*

They were screening *Gentlemen Prefer Blondes*. It was the first time I ever saw Marilyn on a big screen. I knew who she was – can't grow up and not recognise that face. But that day was the first time I'd ever seen her in motion. Talk about being hypnotised.

It was the same day as Mum's funeral. Gran didn't think I should go to the crem, but I look back now and think eleven's old enough to say goodbye. It was Gran who couldn't face going really, she let Grandad take care of everything. But it was a treat to go to the flicks, in a weird way. Cos, ironically, Mum would never have been caught dead there.

Mum didn't go into town. Said you'd catch a disease, or worse – a filthy idea. Made us live like ghosts in that flat. Curtains drawn. Only way the world could get to us was through the telly. I mean, she wasn't daft, was she? The outside world will do you in one way or another. But back then, I swore if Mum was gonna live in the shadows, I was gonna live in the flashbulb.

Every Friday, we'd have fish and chips. Mum would send me down there with fifty pence to get a large cod to share. One Friday, I was in a foul mood. Maybe cos it was April and still snowing. Usually, I'd bite her hand off at a chance to escape, but I refused to go. Said if she wanted chips that bad, she should get 'em herself. Thought a bit of tough love might help. Or maybe I was just being a little cow. Either way, I couldn't believe my eyes when she grabbed her coat.

She got hit crossing the road, by a Volvo doing forty-two in a thirty. Dead before she hit the tarmac. The next day, her blood was still there. Turning all slushy with the melting ice. Grandad tried to hose it away, but. I had to go out with a scrubbing brush in the end.

As we left the cinema, we took a walk along the sea front. That's when Gran told me Marilyn grew up without her mum, too. It all made sense. That's why Marilyn looked straight down the lens and reached for me. Held my hand through the whole picture.

Like Gran said. *'You and her. You've got that same stardust, darlin'.'* Turns out stardust burns up pretty quickly.

She places the cinema ticket down, goes to throw the packaging of her delivery in the bin. Only, she discovers a Post-it note stuck to the back.

She reads it. Panic rising.

Fuck. It's the wolves, Bobby.

Scene Four – *"The River of No Return"*

Night. **Denise** *in a spotlight.*

A cheap backing track crackles through a worn-out speaker, tinny and strained. **Denise** *sings along to 'The River of No Return'. As the song progresses she grips the mic a little tighter, spotting something in the audience. Her knuckles whitening. A deer caught in the headlights. But she carries on, determined to finish her act.*

The speaker crackles and cuts out.

Lights.

Scene Five – *"Wolves I Have Known"*

Night. Lake Mead. **Denise** *pours herself a brandy.*

Denise   Five words on that Post-it, Bobby. *'Cops called. Looking for you.'* My fault. This is what happens when you let your guard down, make connections.

She turns toward the vivarium.

Oh, don't look like that. I know, I've got you. But it's not the same. I should've moved us on weeks ago. Told you someone was watching. But I've handled it. Things will blow over. It's not really that bad up here by Lake Mead, is it?

She steels herself.

S'not like I didn't think about getting out of the state all together. We've had other false alarms. But what about the audition tomorrow? Legends Reborn. I have to stay. If they catch me now . . .

They catch me as nobody.

Beat.

And I've been thinking. They can't know everything, can they? If they did . . .

It's best not to spook the horses. That's why I used everything Marilyn's taught me tonight.

The gig was a shitty dinner show. Overcooked $45 steak, no one listening. I was halfway through River of No Return before I spotted him. This wolf. Lounging at the back. Helping himself to the free olives.

I've met all kinds of wolves in my time. But this one . . . Detective Delfino. He's the kind who lets you finish your eleven o'clock number before he strikes.

Marilyn wrote about them, you know. The wolves she'd known. Men who waited in the wings for her, teeth bared and their ties neat. But I've got this wolf wrapped 'round my little finger. Poor sod. Fluttered my eyelashes, and his brain short-circuited.

I'll give him this – the detective does have presence. Jaded, cynical, like he was bullied at school and never really got over it. He's Texan.

Just like Cody. That deep, sexy drawl. Hair slicked back. Huge arms. Smoked rollies like he was waiting for *Ginsberg* to put him in a poem.

I met him two weeks after turning sixteen. I was working as a shot girl at Hollywood's in Romford. They never asked about my age, and I looked way older. Gran and Grandad thought I worked down the amusements. S'pose I did. At the weekends, you'd have like two thousand sweaty bodies all pressed up against each other.

Cody was such a sexy dancer. The fucking was constant. Makes me sound like a twat, but it was like a lightning bolt. The love for him was there all at once, all consuming. Gran dropped one of her crystal ashtrays when she found out he was thirty-two. Said he was a dirty old sod. But I've never been good at hearing no.

He was only over here for the summer. Visiting an army mate he'd met during a stint in West Germany. But he doted on me – drove me all over London, chasing open calls and doorstepping casting directors. I'd queue for hours in the rain with my portfolio in a Safeway bag. I got a few gigs as a background dancer. You can see me in a Velvet Hush video. Blue bikini. Got a fiver and a donner kebab for the day's work.

I knew I'd have to give up and get a proper job eventually, but Cody kept saying my big break would come. It was just a matter of time. What a cunt.

By the end of summer, he was heading back to America. Insisted I should come with him. I thought he was taking the piss – another one of his windups. But this time, he was dead serious. He had a mate in Hollywood who was making movies. He could pull a few strings for me.

The plan was, we'd drive across country from his parents' aloe vera farm in Texas. Wind our way through cowboy towns – Amarillo, Cripple Creek. Places where people reinvent themselves. I thought that sounded wonderful.

'What's keeping you in South End?' he kept asking. Cody was right; I needed to get out. I'd have thrown myself off the pier already if it wasn't a mile's walk to the end.

When I told Gran and Grandad, they went ballistic. Said if I got on that plane, I'd be flushing my whole life down the shitter. Grandad screamed in my face, *'You go with him, don't bother coming back.'*

'Have it your way, I s'pose.'

At least I was true to my word. Course, as soon as the plane landed, Cody told me he didn't really wanna go to LA. He was thinking of staying in Texas, helping out more on the Aloe farm.

'It's good honest work, Denise.' But I didn't come all that way for soil and sweat. I had a destiny. I got my way in the end, but only if I paid for the gas.

End of the first week on the road, Cody confesses his mate doesn't actually *make* movies, he just rents traffic cones out to studios. Says he's *connected*, like that means anything. But Marilyn wouldn't have let a thing like that stop her.

Beat.

We never even made it as far as Albuquerque. His dad's battered truck started playing up, started coughing filth. My fault, obviously. We ended up pulling into this grim little motel. Looked like somewhere Norman Bates would get a stiffy for.

I'd felt rough all day. Been sick a couple of times at the side of the road. I still felt dizzy as I sat in the motel bar, sipping a warm beer. As I finished the bottle, I realised.

I was late.

Debated telling him. Thought maybe it was smarter to keep it to myself a few days – come up with a plan, in case he flipped.

But there was this kamikaze part of me that couldn't hold it in. I wanted to see if he'd be happy. Like I was. I wanted him to choose me. The whole situation. Right there and then.

He didn't say anything. Paced around the tiny room, wearing a hole in the carpet. Chain smoking. He told me he loved me. Went to the bathroom and washed his face. I thought I might have heard him crying, but sometimes I can't trust my imagination. Or my memory. Or both. Anyway, he reappeared, picked up the car keys, told me he was gonna get beers. Did I want anything? A piece of fruit. He said he wouldn't be long.

That was it. He never came back. He took the car, the money, my clothes. Left me without a passport. With nothing.

I spent a few nights in the Greyhound station. Eventually hustled enough change for a one-way ticket to LA. Walked up and down Hollywood Boulevard until my feet blistered. Finally, I found this all-night diner with a sign in the window: *Kitchen help wanted. No time-wasters.*

How could I bring a baby into that, Bobby?

Beat.

Three months later, a regular said his sister did catering for film sets and they always needed someone to scrape plates. It was a way in. Every so often, I'd catch a glimpse of a monitor. Some starlet in full make-up. I was only thirty feet away.

I'm not stupid. I don't tell Delfino any of this when he asks how I got to the States. I keep it breezy, tell him I'd originally been a nanny for a family in Pasadena. And when he goes on, asks me if I ever worked for the King, I play dumb.

'Of England? It's not like we've all got him on speed dial, you know.'

'Elvis,' he says. *'Well, Vegas's answer to him. Dwayne Quinn.'*

He lets the name hang there, waiting for me to flinch.

'Worked for him, did you? At the Golden Pyramid?'

I act like I've got nothing to hide.

'Yeah, I helped with costumes. Quit 'cos he kept making me measure his inside leg.'

I throw that in just to make Delfino squirm.

Then I give him something – tell him I heard Dwayne packed it in years ago. Selling palm trees now, apparently.

Delfino smiles, satisfied. Thank God. *'Don't worry. All routine. Checking a few names on a list. You understand.'*

I smile back. Lashes and lipstick. Nothing to see here. Held my nerve, Bobby, and he bought it. Wolves always think they've won when you let them leave with their pride intact.

He *wants* me to be harmless. And that's good, Bobby. Very good.

Scene Six – *"The Hollywood Years"*

Morning. The radio is playing. **Denise** *is in the bathroom.*

Radio News Report   *'Breaking this morning – police are investigating a headless corpse found in a shallow grave near the San Gabriel Mountains. A hiker discovered the body last Friday. Detectives say the man may have been buried for decades and are appealing for information –'*

Denise (*off*)   *Fuck!*

Denise *enters, switches the radio off. A lipstick smear on her face.*

Denise   No more distractions. How many times have I drawn this face? And now my hands won't stop shaking. Lips like a clown on ket.

She looks in her compact mirror.

Jesus. Why'd I ever wanna grow old without surgery? Being loyal to the face I've got was a mistake. I wish I was more like Gran. *'Every face becomes a skull'* was her motto.

Beat.

At least they'll never find the head.

I need water.

She grabs a bottle of sparkling water from her battered mini fridge.

I've always hated auditions, Bobby. Getting in the room was never the problem. I could blag past security, flirt with a line producer, find out where I needed to be.

But every time I opened my mouth, I blew it. My words would get tangled. *Spark,* but no timing. Looks, but no charisma. I knew I was fucking it up. Like there was a better version of me just outside my reach, and I couldn't get hold of her.

I did okay with commercial gigs. My first real job was this cigarette ad. *Smoke Like a Lady.* Black and white. Tight curls, cocktail dress. I still have one of the posters somewhere. All I had to do was walk across the room, sit down, and spark up. I was fucking marvellous.

'Want me to say anything?' I asked, trying not to get ash on my shoes.

'God no.'

The director was called Ray. Seemed nice enough. Had a ponytail, which never looks good on a man. That gig led to a cereal box in Denmark. The dizzying heights of a student film or two. But there's only so many years you can slog through shit before you begin to wonder if you're the problem.

I remember asking Ray once. Told him to be honest. Always a mistake. Said I was believable in a role 'til I opened my mouth. I begged him for something bigger, a real part. I'd already given up too much – my best years, Gran and Grandad, a baby.

Marilyn never got to be a mother either. Denied it, like me. All that wanting and nowhere for it to go. It hollows you out.

I told Ray everything one night, after too many margaritas. Think he didn't know what to say, so he offered me a part. A straight-to-TV magician murder mystery. Lit like a brothel, plot thinner than a playing card. But he was excited about the big trick at the end.

I was in this sequined leotard, had to step into a magic cabinet. And when they opened the doors – ta-dah! There's a giant snake in my place. Magic.

I was introduced to the snake, who I might add, had a bigger dressing room than I did. She was a seventeen-foot-long reticulated python called Susan. Terrifying. I know, Bobby, but back then I was uneducated.

There was a bigger problem than Susan. The fucking trick. The bolt was sticky, so the hidden panel wouldn't budge the first time. They open the cabinet for the big reveal – and there I am, still inside, scrabbling around like a twat.

Ray loses it. We reset. This time I nail it. Slick exit, perfect timing. But Ray? He doesn't let me out. Or answer when I call. No one does. I hear the crew pack up and leave.

I stayed in that box. All night. Trapped. With the snake.

I pissed myself I was that scared. But Susan never hurt me. She curled round my ankles. Waited. You see, when a woman teams up with a snake, a storm always follows – just ask Eve.

Beat.

Ray finally shows up the next morning, unlocks the box – Susan goes straight for him. The sound he made, like a dog caught in barbed wire. He staggered back, grabbing at her, but she was wrapped tight, jaws locked. Blood pouring down his elbow, splattering the dolly.

The crew scrambled, knocking over light-stands. Someone called 911. But Susan didn't let go. Not 'til he went limp.

Watta girl.

Beat.

Turns out, locking a girl in a box was just the warm-up act. Ray went on to be one of those monsters they make documentaries about now. Everyone saying he hid his deviance. But not that well, Bobby.

Might've stopped him then. Just needed someone to say, '*Hey – maybe don't lock the actress in a box with a fucking python?*'

Beat. She shrugs.

Anyway, Ray comes to in the hospital, raving that I set Susan on him. The snake handler was distraught. Word quickly got round and it wasn't long before the city ordered Susan be put down. But not before I saved her child. You, my beautiful, Bobby.

A shit end for your mummy. But if anyone's gonna help you through life – should be someone who's already crawled through it.

She puts her hand on the glass of the vivarium.

I had a lot of time to think in that box. I realised: Hollywood was never gonna love me. So, I stopped asking. And Marilyn's untouchable, isn't she? That's all I ever really wanted. A bit of sparkle between me and the truth. She let me matter in a world that didn't care if I vanished.

And today's the day. I won't mess this audition up like I used to.

Time to sparkle.

Scene Seven – *"The Audition"*

Denise *stands with a mobile pressed to her ear. She's somewhere else – an audition space, even outside – but it's not the motorhome.*

Voicemail (*of Joanie Fontaine*)   *Hey – you've reached Joanie Fontaine. If this is Liza, I'll call you back. If it's not, good luck.*

Beep.

Denise *launches into a diatribe – speaks directly, urgently.*

Denise   Joanie. It's Denise. Just got here. Some child in a headset tells me the Marilyn section's been cut. Cut! Apparently, she's not got the pull. Not like Elvis. Or Springsteen. Are you having a fucking laugh?

You wanna talk about irrelevant? Irrelevant is spotlighting every bloke in a jumpsuit and binning the woman who invented icon. She dragged herself out of an orphanage, built her own studio when no one thought a woman could, stood up for Black performers – and died with a belly full of drugs and no one to hold her hand.

And you're saying she doesn't matter? I'm sixty-one, Joanie. Spent thirty years perfecting her. I've been Marilyn longer than she ever got to be. But now I'm the wrong kind of nostalgia?

Marilyn walked so half your fucking line-up could strut. Without her, there's no Madonna. Or Cher. No drag brunch at the Flamingo. She made blonde mean something.

She pauses. Eyes stinging, but her voice stays strong.

You know what, I'm glad I'll have nothing to do with this sad little enterprise. You're a fool, Joanie. You've just taken the soul out the whole fucking show.

She stabs the phone off.

Scene Eight – *"Elvis"*

Morning. The motorhome.

Denise *sits.*

Denise   Detective Delfino is back. Says it's definitely
Dwayne in the grave. DNA confirms it. They're horrified
someone took the head. He was buried in his Elvis jumpsuit
– what's left of it. Just scraps of white fabric now, gold
rhinestones. The wig was in there too.

They traced the fabric to a shop on Rancho Drive. I could
never afford to shop there now, Bobby, but back in the day?
It was the only place you could get stuff that didn't wash out
under the lights. Double-weight satin charmeuse. Bone-lined
zippers.

The shop stopped carrying the fabric years ago. But they
remembered who used to buy it. In bulk.

Beat.

Elvis always said you should look your best for your big
number. That meant no poly blends. Everything had to be
lined in champagne or midnight blue. But he let me go wild
everywhere else, so long as it screamed Presley. Flames on
his trousers. Collars so wide you could lose a gospel choir
behind them.

She smiles.

The first Marilyn outfit I ever made, though. Off-white
nylon, twenty-two per cent stretch. Vile.

My friend Heaven gave me the gig. She did a mean Cher –
said the trick was to sing from the throat not the soul.
Heaven ran this little touring tribute night, and their Stevie
Nicks had dropped out after falling awkwardly on her
tambourine. So, there was a gap. And I was born ready.

I wasn't polished, not yet. But something cracked open in
me. Even in a room of ten people on happy hour whiskey, I
made them believe. I was an apparition. The most important

thing those six months on the road with Heaven taught me, was what I value most in life. A set of wheels.

One night, we did a gig at the Burbank Ramada. I'm halfway through 'Diamonds are a Girl's Best Friend' when I spot him in the audience. Black aviators. Sideburns sculpted like a Roman bust. The other impersonators tell me he used to be one of them, but he now drives a white Cadillac and headlines in Vegas.

Backstage, Elvis hands me a martini. Looks me up and down. Not in a pervy way – more like he's looking at a painting that's not quite finished, but he knows exactly how I'll look hanging in his casino lobby.

And fuck, can the man talk. And that's coming from *me*. He's off on one telling me how he's gonna make his real fortune in palm trees. Build a legacy, one frond at a time.

'You ever been to Vegas?' he asked.

I told him I didn't think the strip would suit me. He smiled like he'd already decided otherwise.

Then came the pitch. *'The Golden Pyramid. You as Marilyn. For a full season. What d'ya say, kid?'*

Beat.

I wish I'd never laid eyes on Elvis Presley.

Delfino says the cops are confused. Cos, they found the jumpsuit, the jewellery, even the fucking wig. But no sign of the black aviators.

'Funny,' Delfino said. *'Man never took them off.'*

I told him maybe the coyotes nicked 'em.

But he clocked something in my face. I know he did.

'I dunno. Figure whoever sawed off his head musta kept 'em as a trophy. The killer's probably a bit of a collector.'

He said he'd be back. With a warrant.

Scene Nine – "*Run*"

Night. The motorhome. Everything's chaos. **Denise**, *wild-eyed.*

Denise (*to* **Bobby**)   Heat lamp. Spare bulbs. Water dish, travel tank, your calming towel.

She puts down her list.

Right, sweetie. This is it. You and me, we start again.

New name. New town. I've been toying with Ruth, or Velma. Although maybe neither of them suit me.

She takes out a bag from somewhere, starts counting cash.

Always knew this day would come, but it's over. Unless we run. It's the only way. We tried, Bobby. But the curtain's coming down.

She tries to cram the cash into a suitcase. The zip snaps. Feathers and rhinestones explode out.

The phone begins to ring. She stares at it, worried, but picks up.

Hello? Speaking. Oh – Joanie. Hi.

Beat.

No, I just didn't expect . . .

A longer beat.

Yes. She is the soul of the show. Glad you agree.

Her face changes – not panic, not relief. Just sorrow.

That's kind of you. Of course, I'm honoured. It's perfect. It's just . . .

Her voice breaks.

I can't. You're gonna have to find someone else.

She hangs up. Sits down. Slowly. In the middle of the wreckage.

Scene Ten – *"Bye Bye Bobby"*

Night. **Denise** *sits at the table. A battered tape recorder, and the pair of black aviators she was wearing at the beginning are in front of her. She presses record.*

Denise (*into recorder*)   This is for you, Detective Delfino.

I know you'll be back. Ready to box everything up, like it's junk. Shove it in some sad storage unit. But this isn't evidence. I built it. Piece by piece. With everything I had. And you don't get to take it from me.

Beat.

My name is Denise Jarvis. And I killed a man who promised me everything. You have to know, Dwayne said my dreams would come true. But headliners don't sign contracts with no exit clause. Work double shows, six nights a week, for nothing.

I was one of twelve Marilyns. A chorus-line of blondes, all doing the same routine in heels that barely fit. The weekly infected blisters. I'd made it to Vegas, but I was on stage for two minutes – downstage left, behind the speaker. And the lead Marilyn was tone deaf. Took everything I had not to go full Tonya Harding.

I was sewing all the girls' costumes too – not just for our number, the whole company. For no extra. Not that I was being paid anyway. Every time I asked Dwayne, all I got was: *'It's coming, darlin'.'*

Bullshit. I was trapped. No way back to LA. I lived in my car for a year. Learned every parking lot in Nevada. Stole leftover food at the casino. I'd like to see how long you'd manage.

Beat.

The gun was just to threaten him into giving me what I was owed. But Dwayne didn't scare easy. Said I was nothing before him and I'd be nothing without him. I don't know who reached first. Who shoved. But either way the gun went off.

She lets it sit.

I dragged him to his Cadillac. Drove out past the San Gabriel Mountains. I told myself I was tucking him in for the night. But I couldn't leave him with his face. His smile. Those fucking sunglasses still on.

I needed to make him smaller. Consolidate the problem.

First, I wrapped a towel round his head. But the blade stuck – wouldn't go in clean. I had to push down with my whole bodyweight. I remember the sound. Something between a branch snapping and a kiss.

I thought it would be fast. It wasn't. The neck. The jaw. The soft bits went first. Then cartilage. Bone. You don't think about how much holds a head in place.

Beat.

I fed him to my snake. Bobby. He regurgitated the teeth and the hair.

*She exhales. Presses stop. Ejects the tape. Then turns to **Bobby**, in his tank.*

Denise   You beautiful boy. You seemed to really enjoy his eyeballs.

Beat.

But you never asked to be part of this. I made you an accomplice. And I'm sorry. I promised your mother I'd take care of you. But I dragged you into something awful. It ends now.

She snaps the tape in two. Tosses it in the bin. Silence.

Denise *opens a small can of petrol. Begins to pour it around the motorhome. Steady. Focused.*

It's done. I can't keep wearing her skin. But how am I supposed to be Denise again? Next time, hopefully I'll just be someone quiet. Someone who keeps chickens. But. Whoever it is, wherever it is, Bobby – you can't come. It's not fair to have a witness this time.

She reaches for the lid of the vivarium. Hesitates. This is hard.

I think you should see the stars tonight.

She takes the lid off.

Don't be scared. The desert's tough. Unforgiving. You might think you won't survive. But you will.

She sings to him.

Denise *begins to sing 'Bye Bye Baby' from Gentlemen Prefer Blondes.*

She takes the Formosa Café matchbook she placed on the shelf earlier. Strikes one. The flash of a flame –

Blackout.

Methuen Drama Modern Plays

include

Bola Agbaje
Ayad Akhtar
Edward Albee
Jean Anouilh
John Arden
Peter Barnes
Clare Barron
Sebastian Barry
Alistair Beaton
Brendan Behan
Edward Bond
William Boyd
Bertolt Brecht
Howard Brenton
Amelia Bullmore
Anthony Burgess
Leo Butler
Jim Cartwright
Lolita Chakrabarti
Caryl Churchill
Lucinda Coxon
Tim Crouch
Shelagh Delaney
Ishy Din
Claire Dowie
David Edgar
David Eldridge
Dario Fo
Michael Frayn
John Godber
James Graham
David Greig
John Guare
Lauren Gunderson
Peter Handke
David Harrower
Jonathan Harvey
Robert Holman
David Ireland
Sarah Kane

Barrie Keeffe
Jasmine Lee-Jones
Anders Lustgarten
Duncan Macmillan
David Mamet
Patrick Marber
Martin McDonagh
Alistair McDowall
Arthur Miller
Tom Murphy
Phyllis Nagy
Anthony Neilson
Peter Nichols
Ben Okri
Joe Orton
Vinay Patel
Joe Penhall
Luigi Pirandello
Stephen Poliakoff
Lucy Prebble
Peter Quilter
Mark Ravenhill
Philip Ridley
Willy Russell
Sam Shepard
Martin Sherman
Chris Shinn
Jackie Sibblies Drury
Wole Soyinka
Simon Stephens
Kae Tempest
Laura Wade
Anne Washburn
Timberlake Wertenbaker
Roy Williams
Snoo Wilson
Theatre Workshop
Frances Ya-Chu Cowhig
Benjamin Zephaniah

For a complete listing of
Methuen Drama titles, visit:

www.bloomsbury.com/drama

Follow us on X and keep up to date with
our news and publications

@MethuenDrama